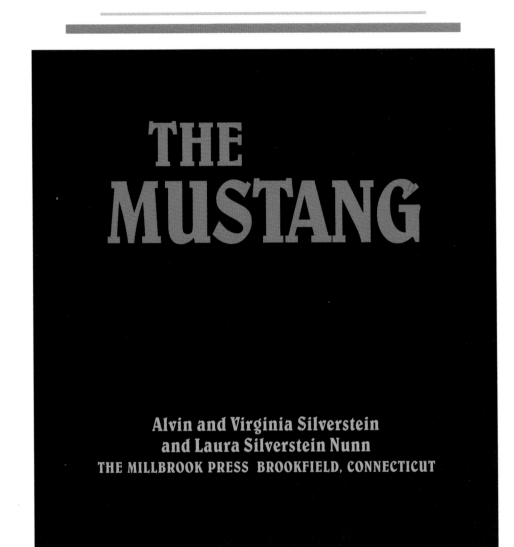

THE
MUSTANG

**Alvin and Virginia Silverstein
and Laura Silverstein Nunn**
THE MILLBROOK PRESS BROOKFIELD, CONNECTICUT

Cover photograph courtesy of Photo Researchers (© Renee Lynn).
Photographs courtesy of Animals, Animals: pp. 4
(© Yva Momatiuk & John Eastcott), 49 (© John Eastcott & Yva
Momatiuk); The National Audubon Society Collection/Photo Researchers: pp. 9, 20 (© Elisabeth Weiland), 25 (© 1991 Tom & Pat Leeson), 27
(© 1988 William Munoz); Bob Goodman: pp. 15 (© 1993), 33 (©
1987); Joan Bolsinger: p. 39; AP/Wide World Photos: p. 41; BLM-Reno:
p. 47 (Susan Bowlus); Susanne Edler: p. 51; Sygma: p. 55 (© J.L. Atlan).

Library of Congress Cataloging-in-Publication Data
Silverstein, Alvin.
The mustang / by Alvin and Virginia Silverstein
and Laura Silverstein Nunn.
p. cm. — (Endangered in America)
Includes bibliographical references (p.   ) and index.
Summary: Describes the habits and habitats of wild mustangs and
the efforts being made to save these horses from extinction.
ISBN 0-7613-0048-1
1. Mustang—Juvenile literature. 2. Wild horses—West (U.S.)—
Juvenile literature. [1. Mustang. 2. Wild horses. 3. Horses.
4. Endangered species.] I. Silverstein, Virginia B. II. Nunn, Laura
Silverstein. III. Title. IV. Series: Silverstein, Alvin.
Endangered in America.
SF293.M9S55 1997 599.72′5—dc20 96–42682 CIP AC

Published by The Millbrook Press, Inc.
2 Old New Milford Road, Brookfield, Connecticut 06804

CONTENTS

Wild horses—traditional symbol of our Western heritage—running through Green River Basin, Wyoming.

AMERICA'S LIVING LEGEND

Imagine thousands of wild horses thundering across the open lands of the Old West. Those wild horses are also called mustangs. They are so much a part of our image of the Old West that it seems hard to believe they are not really wild. They are not even native to America. The mustangs are descendants of horses that were brought to the New World by Spanish explorers hundreds of years ago and of various breeds of horses turned loose by ranchers and farmers.

Mustangs have become America's most famous horses. They are associated with many of the people and events in America's history: the Indian warriors of the Plains, the cavalry battles of the Civil War, the Pony Express, the stagecoach era, and the cowboys of the West. As the United States became more modernized, however, the mustang became less useful. The horses were viewed as a nuisance, and they were hunted and killed.

As they moved into mustang territories, farmers and ranchers were angry that the wild horses were eating the grasses that could be used by livestock. They also claimed that the horses were over-grazing and destroying the land. As a result, thousands of mustangs were rounded up and slaughtered. The Bureau of Land Management (BLM), a government agency, was in charge of the public lands, and the ranchers paid a fee for their livestock to graze on them. When the ranchers complained about the mustangs, the BLM allowed the ranchers to get rid of the horses. The number of wild horses dwindled drastically, from an estimated 2 million in 1860 to only 17,000 mustangs in 1970.

PROTECTING THE HORSES

In the early 1970s, people throughout America became concerned over the plight of the mustangs. Animal groups were certain that these horses—a vivid symbol of the nation's history—would become extinct within a decade. The mustang was discussed on radio and television and in schools throughout the country. Congress received thousands of letters, mostly from schoolchildren, about saving the mustangs. The efforts of these children helped to give the mustangs a chance to prosper again. In 1971, Congress passed the Wild Free-Roaming Horse and Burro Act, which, among other things, made it illegal to harass or kill wild horses or burros on public lands.

In the mid-1970s, ranchers complained to the BLM that the wild-horse populations were rapidly increasing by as much as 20 percent each year. The ranchers put pressure on the BLM to reduce the numbers of wild horses. To protect the horses, new legislation set up an Adopt-A-Horse program, which was a good idea but full of problems. The BLM rounded up thousands of horses for the program. At first, about 10 percent of them were severely injured or killed during the roundups. As the BLM improved their practices, the Adopt-A-Horse program found homes for many wild horses. Other efforts to control the number of wild horses have included private sanctuaries and experimental fertility programs.

With legal protection, the mustangs continued to thrive and multiply. Not only were America's wild horses no longer in danger, but in some areas they were too numerous—more than the land could support. Today, opinions differ about what should be done about the mustangs. Some people believe that wild horses are ruining the land, and their numbers must be controlled. On the other hand, animal-protection groups argue that livestock outnumber mustangs by more than 100 to 1 and that the livestock are more likely to damage the land. Some ecologists say that the huge expenses required to manage mustangs would be better spent protecting endangered species. While the debate continues, the fate of America's wild horses hangs in the balance.

HORSES IN HISTORY

Horses have been around since prehistoric times. The first horses originated in North America about 60 million years ago. There were land bridges between continents at that time, which later allowed the horse to spread to Asia, Europe, and Africa. Scientists call these early horses *Eohippus* ("dawn horse"). *Eohippus* was a very small animal, standing only 10 to 20 inches (25 to 50 centimeters) tall. It looked more like a racing dog, such as a greyhound, than the modern horse we know today.

NORTH AMERICAN HORSES DISAPPEAR

About 3 million years ago, the *Eohippus* evolved into *Equus*, the genus to which the modern horse belongs. *Equus* thrived until about 8,000 years ago, when, along with other mammals, it mysteriously disappeared from the North American continent during the Ice Age. Some people theorize that the climatic changes caused the animals to become extinct. Ecologist Paul S. Martin believes that Stone Age hunters, who killed them for food, hunted them out of existence.

The prehistoric *Eohippus*, an early ancestor of the modern horse, was a small animal, similar in size to a dog.

The only horses left were those in Asia, Europe, and Africa. Eventually, people started to tame these wild horses instead of hunting them. The horses were used to carry heavy equipment and supplies, as well as human riders. On horseback, people could travel farther and faster than they could on foot. In battle, warriors on horseback could easily conquer tribes that did not have horses.

In different regions, people bred horses for different tasks. In Europe, domestic horses tended to be large and strong, bred to pull heavy loads and carry knights in their heavy metal armor. The Moors (the Arabs of North Africa) bred their horses for beauty and speed, producing a breed now known as the Barb. These North

African horses were small but rugged, able to survive in the hot deserts of North Africa.

When the Moors invaded Spain in the early 700s, their fast horses outperformed the slow and heavy horses of the defending Spaniards, and the Moors conquered much of Spain. The Spaniards, impressed by the beauty and resourcefulness of the Moors' horses, tried to improve their own breeds. They bred North African Barbs with some of their own, larger horses. The result was a breed called the Jennet, which is a bit larger than the Barb, but extremely fast and intelligent.

HORSES RETURN TO AMERICA

In the late-fifteenth century, Christopher Columbus carried horses with him during his second voyage to the New World. Later explorers took horses with them, too, but the Spanish conquistadors were the first to bring horses back to America.

In 1519, Hernando Cortés took sixteen horses along when he sailed from Cuba to Mexico. The horses carried Cortés and his army across Mexico in search of land and gold. With the help of their strong horses, the Spaniards overpowered the Aztecs who inhabited the land. As the Spaniards settled in the New World, they brought over more horses from Spain—so many that the Spanish rulers worried about whether enough would be left for the needs of Spain. Eventually, exporting horses was forbidden. But horse-breeding farms had already been set up in the newly established West Indian colonies of Cuba, Puerto Rico, and Santo Domingo.

Some of the Spanish horses in Mexico escaped or were abandoned. These horses roamed free in the wild. They established herds and multiplied. These were America's first mustangs.

THE VALUE OF HORSES

The Spanish settlers forced Native Americans to work at the missions and ranches. The Native Americans were frightened at first, because they had never seen horses before. They thought that the horses with their riders were four-legged monsters.

Soon, however, the Native Americans noticed that these "beasts" obeyed the commands of the Spanish riders. Once they realized how useful horses could be, many Native Americans hopped on the horses in the middle of the night and rode away. Often, they returned to the ranches and missions and captured more horses. Members of other tribes soon traded beads and furs for horses. Because of this horse trading, mustangs gradually moved northward to the Rocky Mountains and into Canada. Some ran away or were turned loose, which added to the growing wild herds.

Horses greatly changed the way of life for many western tribes. Native Americans used horses for traveling and for hunting buffalo. The horses also helped the tribes to battle each other and the invading settlers.

During the 1600s and 1700s, settlers from Spain moved into Florida, and others from Mexico moved into California. In 1775, Spanish settlers took more than 500 horses to the San Francisco Bay area. By 1800 many of these horses had formed wild herds. The

The Mustangs of North Carolina

WHEN PEOPLE HEAR the word "mustang," they think of the Old West, but herds of mustangs are still living today on islands off the southeastern coast of the United States. The wild horse herds of the Outer Banks, a chain of narrow sand islands and peninsulas along the coast of North Carolina, are descended from horses brought by Spanish explorers in 1523. The Spaniards began to establish a colony there but never completed it. When they left, the horses remained.

In the 1700s, English settlers used the island horses for transportation, rounding up livestock, and pulling fishing nets. In the 1800s, the U.S. Life Saving Service used the mustangs for beach patrol. During the Depression of the 1930s, the wild horses were sold as a source of income. Today the Corolla Wild Horse Fund on Currituck Beach has established a nonprofit Wild Horse Sanctuary to protect the mustangs that remain there.

land provided plenty of water, grassland, and territory, so the California mustangs flourished and soon numbered in the thousands.

In the early 1800s it was estimated that 1 to 2 million mustangs roamed the Great Plains and deserts. Mustangs became so numerous that areas of the Southwest were labeled as "Wild Horse Desert" on maps.

Meanwhile, settlers from the eastern states were moving westward in search of more land for homesteads. Gradually, they established farms, ranches, and towns in the midwestern and western states. They fenced off areas that Native Americans considered traditional hunting grounds, so battles between the tribes and the settlers became common. Most mustangs of the Great Plains were horses that had escaped during these battles or during horse raids.

Early in the nineteenth century, settlers from the eastern states moved across the Great Plains. By the 1880s, the last Native Americans were forced out of the territory and onto reservations. Many of their horses were left behind and joined others in the wild.

THE ROLE OF MUSTANGS IN HISTORY

Cowboys became popular during the 1860s through the 1880s. These were men who helped take care of herds of cattle for ranchers. They often rode mustangs, which made excellent "cow ponies."

Mustangs were sturdy workhorses, too. Farmers used them to pull heavy wagons and plows. The famous Pony Express used fast, sturdy horses to deliver mail across the country. Horse-drawn stagecoaches were the main form of long-distance transportation for passengers.

By the 1900s, however, horses were becoming less useful. Trains, tractors, trucks, and automobiles took over the work of transportation and hauling. The mustang was soon viewed as nothing more than a pest.

WHAT IS A MUSTANG?

Many people think that the terms "mustang" and "wild horse" refer to the same animal. Mustangs roam freely in the wild, but they are not true wild horses. They are actually feral (untamed) animals, descendants of domesticated (tamed) horses that escaped or were released into the wild. The ancestors of the first mustangs were domesticated horses brought to the New World by the Spanish explorers. The Spanish horses that ran away to live in the wild were called "mustangs," which is the English pronunciation of the Spanish word *mesteño* (mess-ten-yo), meaning "stray" or "wild." These wild horses are grazing animals that depend primarily on grass and water. Today mustangs can be found in herds on public lands in ten western states, especially in the Great Basin desert of Nevada.

Mustangs are generally smaller than domestic horses. They weigh about 1,000 pounds (450 kilograms) or less. A domestic horse can weigh about 1,200 pounds (545 kilograms) or more. Many mustangs are smaller than domestic horses because they have difficulty finding enough food to eat. Domestic horses are usually fed well by their owners.

The height of a horse is measured in hands. One hand is equal to 4 inches (10 centimeters). A mustang usually grows to about 14

Mustangs, with various colorings and patterns of colors, grazing in Amargosa Valley, Nevada.

hands (56 inches, or about 142 centimeters) tall at the withers (the area between the shoulders), but a mustang's height can vary greatly—from 3 feet (0.9 meter) to more than 5 feet (1.5 meters).

Mustangs can be a variety of colors and patterns of colors. Some of the most common colors are bay (reddish brown coat), sorrel (yellowish brown coat), dun (yellowish gray), chestnut, black, and gray. The roan has a solid-colored coat and white hairs scattered over the body. The palomino is golden-colored with a white

Mustangs Are Tough

EVEN THOUGH MUSTANGS are smaller than domestic horses, they are not weak or frail. In fact, because mustangs live in such harsh environments in the wild, their experiences have made them tough and sturdy. They are fast and have especially sharp senses, always alert to danger.

In the summer, they must travel through the hot desert sun—without trees to use as shade—in search of water. They dig with their hoofs into the mud of dried-up water-holes. In the winter, the open land offers the horses no protection against the brutal snow-storms. They are then forced to dig into the snow to find frozen clumps of grass to eat. They also have to break the ice on waterholes with their hooves in order to drink.

mane and tail. The buckskin is a yellowish gray. The paint (also called pinto) has a two-colored coat consisting of white and either black or brown. The Appaloosa has a patch of white on the rump with small dark spots.

Mustangs have strong, muscular legs that are perfect for running. They can run as fast as 35 miles (56 kilometers) per hour. The front legs carry most of the horse's weight. The rear legs give the animal power when moving. The horse's foot has only one toe, which is covered by a strong, hard hoof. An elastic mass, called a frog, on the sole of the foot helps to absorb the jolts when the animal runs or jumps. Because mustangs run on rocky ground, their hooves are often much harder and tougher than those of domestic horses. Mustangs have large lungs, which allow them to run for a long time.

The mustang's teeth are perfectly suited for grazing. There are six pairs of small front teeth, called incisors. The incisors are like sharp chisels that can cut tough, stringy grass. The mustang also has twelve pairs of large, flat teeth at the back of its mouth, which are called molars. The molars grind the food as the horse chews. A horse's teeth continue to grow throughout its life, although they are worn down by grazing.

A horse's tail is both attractive and useful. The mustang uses its tail to swat annoying flies.

KEEN SENSES

Horses have highly developed senses of sight, hearing, smell, and touch. These give the animals early warnings of danger. A horse's large eyes can move independently of each other. One eye can look forward while the other one looks backward. This makes it possible for horses to spot objects moving in front of and behind them at a far distance. They can also see fairly well at night.

Horses have small, pointy ears that are highly sensitive to sounds. At the slightest noise, a horse will move its ears in whatever direction the sound is coming from. The outer ear acts like a dish antenna, directing sounds inward to the horse's eardrum.

Horses have large, sensitive nostrils that can detect odors at great distances. They can take in large amounts of air at one time, which provides them with plenty of oxygen when running.

HOW HORSES HAVE CHANGED

Millions of years ago, the horses that roamed the earth were no larger than a small dog. There is a major difference between the modern horse and its distant ancestor, the *Eohippus*. Fossils (ancient skeletons) show that dawn horses did not have hooves like modern horses. They had four toes on their front feet, three toes on their back feet, and arched backs.

Because much of North America was covered with tropical forests and swamps at that time, the dawn horses probably lived in wooded areas and ate leaves. As North America's climate gradually became cooler, the tropical forests and swamps turned into mountains and grassy plains. The dawn horse changed, too. Scientists believe that gradually, over millions of years, the little dawn horse evolved into various types of horses. Some types were still small; others were dramatically larger. The horses adapted to the new environment and changed their ways of living.

Scientists also believe that the changes in the environment and vegetation eventually caused the dawn horses to become extinct. They believe that the horse's body and features were no longer suitable to the environment, and only larger types of horses could survive. As generations went by, horses developed longer legs and became faster runners. According to scientists' theories, the middle toe on each foot carried much of the weight of the animal's heavier body. The side toes gradually became smaller until they disappeared completely, leaving the horse with only one toe on each foot. The horse's single toe evolved into just a toenail, now called a hoof, which is much more suitable for running on hard, dry land.

What Do You Call a Horse?

Colt—technically, a male horse that is less than 4 years old; often used to describe any young horse

Filly—a female horse that is less than 4 years old

Foal—a male or female horse 1 year old or younger

Mare—a female horse that is more than 4 years old

Mustang—wild (feral) horse of the western plains, descended from Spanish horses and ranch stock

Pony—any small horse; specifically, a horse that is less than 58 inches (147 centimeters) tall when fully grown

Stallion—a male horse that can be used for breeding

Yearling—a horse that is more than 1 year old and less than 2 years old

Over time, the horse's neck also changed, and became longer and arched. The teeth became better able to chew grass rather than eat leaves. According to the fossil evidence, about one million years ago, many horses started to look very similar to the modern horses we see today.

REAL WILD HORSES

There have been only two kinds of true wild horses: the Tarpan and Przewalski's horse. The Tarpan, *Equus caballus gmelini,* was a wild horse that lived in forests in Europe and was hunted into extinction in 1860. Przewalski's horse, *Equus przewalskii,* also called the Mongolian wild horse, is the only true wild horse alive today.

Przewalski's horse is short and stocky, standing only 4.5 feet (1.4 meters) tall at the shoulders. It has a large head and a short

The near-extinct Przewalski's horse, also known as the Mongolian wild horse.

black mane that stands erect. Przewalski's horse is closely related to the domestic horse, but it resembles a donkey.

In 1881 a Russian explorer named Nikolai Mikhailovitch Przewalski found the skin and skull of a wild horse in Central Asia. Przewalski believed that the Mongolian wild horse was really a feral horse. He reported his discovery to a zoologist named Y. A. Polyakov, who disagreed with Przewalski's theory. Polyakov was certain that they were primitive wild horses that had survived since the last Ice Age, but no one believed him.

Przewalski's horse received no protection, and the Mongolian wild horses were hunted. By 1920, the wild herds were so diminished that inbreeding was common, and very few pure Przewalski's horses were left. By the time people realized that Polyakov's theory was correct, it was almost too late to save the last true wild horse. Przewalski's horse was then taken into captivity and preserved in zoos and private collections. Unfortunately, Przewalski's horse is believed to be now extinct in the wild. Efforts are now being made to reintroduce some of the horses bred in captivity into part of their former habitat.

AN AMERICAN BREED

Today the American Mustang is a recognized horse breed. For most breeds, there are detailed documents that record centuries of breeding patterns. These records do not exist for the mustang, however. So the American Mustang Association decided instead to use physical characteristics as a way to identify the horses that could be registered as American Mustangs.

The association studied records made by the conquistadors and descriptions by early American writers, as well as woodcuts and other pictures made by artists of those times. This information was compared with material from several South American countries, which were launching programs to preserve feral horses. The descriptions from all these sources were similar and provided the basis for a definition of the breed: a compactly built, well-proportioned, smooth-muscled horse that is strong, agile, intelligent, and adaptable, and that has great endurance and a good disposition.

Some specific features distinguish the American Mustang from other horses: short neck and back; broadly set, alert eyes; straight legs and strong hindquarters, and low-set tail. The American Mustang Association encourages careful breeding of the mustang, to gradually breed out "outside blood" and emphasize the traits of the original Spanish horses.

A MUSTANG'S LIFE

Mustangs are sociable animals. They live in groups, called herds. There are a few different kinds of subgroups in a mustang society.

The most common type is the family band, which usually includes one stallion (adult male horse) and between 1 and 8 mares (adult female horses). Some stallions may gather up to 20 mares. A stallion's collection of mares is called a harem. The family band also includes foals (young male or female horses up to about one year old), colts (male horses under the age of four), and fillies (female horses under the age of four). A family band usually has only one stallion, but there sometimes is more than one. Only one male is dominant, however.

Family bands occasionally meet and graze side by side. Each family band typically roams their own particular territory, called a home range, which averages about 20 square miles (52 square kilometers). A home range must have good grazing areas and sufficient watering places. Mustangs require an average of about 10 to 15 gallons (38 to 57 liters) of water each day (as many as 20 gallons, or 76 liters, in the summer), but they sometimes go without drinking for several days. In the winter and during droughts, food and water are often scarce, and the mustang's home range may expand significantly. In the summer, food and water are usually plentiful, and so mustangs travel shorter distances.

A stallion leads the mustang family band and is known as the band stallion. He is the dominant figure in the herd and is protective of his family. His duties include warning the other horses of approaching danger, fighting battles with rival males, and mating with the mares in the band. The band stallion is also the disciplinarian. If a mare or foal strays too far from the band, the stallion quickly signals a command by lowering his head, stretching his neck, and laying his ears back to tell the horse to get back into the herd. If the command is ignored, the stallion punishes the animal by giving it a little bite on its side.

One of the mares in the herd, usually an older, more experienced female, is second in command to the band stallion. She is known as the lead or alpha mare. When escaping danger, the lead mare takes control of the herd, while the stallion follows. She leads the family band to the safest route and out of danger. The other females in the band understand who the lead mare is and are quick to follow her. She also selects grazing areas and generally is the day-to-day boss.

READY FOR MATING

Horses are usually ready to mate in springtime, although mating can occur at any time of the year. The stallion mates with several mares in his band. Mares usually mate only with the band stallion, but sometimes other males sneak in to mate with the females.

A stallion guarding a mare and her colt in Pryor Mountain Wild Horse Refuge, Wyoming.

About eleven months later, in April or May, mares leave the band and give birth to a single foal in a dark, quiet hiding place. Births usually seem to occur at night or just at dawn. The newborn foals are well developed. After only a few hours, they are able to stand on their own legs and walk around. Soon, the foals can follow their mothers back to the band.

During the first couple of weeks of life, foals feed solely on their mother's milk. When they are three or four weeks old, they start to nibble on grass and nurse less often. Foals no longer depend on their mother's milk by the time they are four to six months old, but they may continue to nurse for up to a year.

A filly is usually ready to mate as a yearling—that is, when she is between one and two years old. If she is still living with her family band, her father will usually chase his daughter away to join another stallion's band. Colts are not ready for breeding until they are two or three years old, and then their fathers force them to leave, too. Some colts may not breed for many years, however, until they are able to win their own mares from the band of another stallion.

BACHELOR BANDS

Colts who are driven away from their family band and males who are unable to win mares for a family band do not live alone. They form their own social group called a bachelor band. These bachelor groups include between 2 and 12 male horses. Members of the bachelor band do not have the responsibilities of those male horses in a family band. They often spend their days grazing, dozing together, and playing games.

One common activity of the bachelor band is called mock fighting. It looks very much like real fighting, but it is only a playful game. The movements of these young stallions are slower than they would be in a real battle. Their bites are only gentle nips, and their kicks never actually touch each other. Mock fighting is helpful to young stallions because it gives them the skills they need to fight other stallions and win mares so that they can form their own family bands.

BATTLING FOR MATES

Stallions often try to gather as many mares as they can by stealing them from another stallion's family band. Sometimes a couple of bachelors will work as a team to take a mare away from the band stallion. While one bachelor picks a fight with the band stallion, the other tries to steal a mare away from the band. When two stallions fight, the battle determines who wins the females. They also fight over grazing land and water.

Stallions in a ritual fighting posture.

Stallions often avoid bloodshed by participating in a practice called ritual posturing. The two stallions face each other with their heads touching so that they are actually breathing into each other's nostrils. As their rage builds, they suddenly toss their heads and neigh angrily, pawing at the ground with their hooves or lashing out with their hind legs. Each horse tries to look as fierce as possible, hoping that the other stallion will be intimidated and run away. The one who stands his ground is the winner of the ritual battle and establishes his dominance.

If neither stallion runs away, the ritual posturing may turn into a vicious battle between the two horses. The fight is often short, but fierce. The mustangs' movements are quick as they let out angry screams, kick each other with their deadly hooves, and bite each other with their sharp teeth. If the defending stallion finally retreats, the winner gathers up as many of his rival's mares as he can for his band and goes on his way. Sometimes the band stallion is so badly wounded that the new stallion takes over the whole band.

RUNNING FROM DANGER

In the past, mustangs had many enemies, including wolves and mountain lions. Today, mustangs have few enemies in the wild. Humans are the most dangerous threat to the mustang.

When mustangs are threatened, they become like a close-knit family, highly dependent upon one another. When the stallion or lead mare spots a hunter or predator, he or she sounds the alarm by snorting loudly to warn the others in the family band. The mares and their young quickly run away, while the stallion follows behind them. Several times, the stallion may stop to face the threat and snort out a warning. Then he turns and urges any lagging band members to run faster. The horses flee to safety in a fast and orderly way, with all the members of the family band keeping their own places in the band.

Mustangs are very fast runners, so running away is usually their best means of defense. Although these horses are usually protective of their offspring, they do not always defend them against predators. Foals that are too slow or weak may be left behind so that the others can escape safely.

MUSTANGS IN DANGER

By 1860, the mustang population reached an all-time high—an estimated 2 million mustangs roamed the West. By the turn of the century, the population was reduced to about 1 million.

When the settlers from the East moved west, they set up ranches and farms that overlapped mustang territory. The ranchers wanted to get rid of the mustangs to make room for their livestock and crops. Some complained that the mustangs were eating grass and drinking water that were meant for their livestock. Others complained that wild stallions were stealing domestic mares and the horses were breaking down fences, allowing livestock to roam freely.

Many ranchers allowed or hired wild-horse hunters, called mustangers, to solve the problem. Mustangers caught so many horses that the mustang population declined drastically.

By 1970, only an estimated 17,000 mustangs remained in the wild. These horses were living in remote areas and were no longer interfering with the cattle ranches. That did not seem to matter to the hunters, however. The mustangers were determined to hunt down every wild horse they could find.

Was it worth it?

The pet-food canneries paid next to nothing for horsemeat. The cost of the fuel used for flying the airplanes was more than the price paid for the horses. Then why did the mustangers have to get "what's still out there"? One mustanger answered this question with another question: "Well, why leave them there? What good are they?"

MUSTANGS AS TARGETS

During the mid-1800s, settlers were determined to chase Native Americans out of the western territory so that they could establish their own communities and make room for their ranches and farms. The settlers quickly learned that the tribesmen's most prized possessions were their horses. By targeting the mustangs, the settlers hoped to overpower the Native Americans and force them out of the western lands.

Although settlers often complained about "Indian horse thieves," the white men actually stole thousands of horses from Native Americans. They herded the horses hundreds of miles across the plains to be sold at auction. Not all the horses made it to their destination in good condition, however. Some became so weak and ill during the trip that they had to be killed. Many of those that survived were driven east, where they were crossbred with American domestic horses, which caused their offspring to lose some of the mustang's Spanish heritage.

MUSTANGS FOR PROFIT

Mustangers were usually hired to corral (capture) the wild horses. They killed many mustangs with their rifles. Other mustangs were rounded up and sent to slaughterhouses, hide buyers, chicken-feed factories, and pet-food canneries. The county governments actively supported the slaughter. Ranchers and mustangers received a reward of two dollars for each pair of horse ears they turned in.

More profits came from the overseas market. Americans sent millions of pounds of horsemeat to Europe, where it was commonly eaten by people. Americans did not feel the same way about eating horsemeat themselves, but in America, thousands of slaughtered horses were used for dogfood.

CORRALLING MUSTANGS

Mustangers can corral wild horses in a variety of ways. In the old days, a mustanger rode on horseback to capture mustangs by running them down and roping them individually. The slow ones were caught easily, whereas the fast ones were difficult to catch. Many got away.

A more effective approach was to chase the horses into a dead-end canyon or a hidden corral. While the horses were trapped with no chance of escape, the mustangers could rope them one at a time.

Another method of corralling wild horses was to build a box trap on a trail used by horse bands. The trap was buried under

Mustangers rounding up horses by
helicopter in Owyhee Desert, Nevada.

loose dirt and leaves and tied to a stone or log. When a horse stepped into the trap, its foot was caught, and it was left behind by the rest of the band. Sometimes traps were built around the waterholes or around springs. Men would hide in trees and drop a gate on any horses that came for a drink.

Mustangers discovered that chasing horses by plane was the easiest method of rounding them up. With the wide, clear view from the air, the mustangers could easily locate the horse bands. Then the airplane, with screaming sirens attached to its wings, would follow the herd. The mustangers would fire gunshots at the horses. The frightened mustangs would run out of their hideaways into the open country, where men in trucks were waiting for them. The horses that refused to leave their hideouts were often shot at with shotguns, and many were blinded. Many horses became so panicked during the stampede that they died from exhaustion.

Once the survivors were corralled, they would often start to fight, pile up, and trample each other to death. The remaining horses, often with severe injuries, were roped and packed tightly into trucks. During the long trip to their destination, the horses were not fed or given water. As a result, this method of corralling caused thousands of injuries and deaths. The horses that survived the trip in fairly good condition were shipped off to dogfood packing plants.

SAVING THE MUSTANG

In 1950, Velma B. Johnston was driving down the highway headed for Reno, Nevada, when she saw a truckload of wild horses. She noticed that there was blood coming out of the trailer, leaving a trail along the road. When the truck stopped, Mrs. Johnston was horrified to see that the horses were in bad shape. They were packed in like sardines. A colt had been trampled to death. Many horses were suffering from gunshot wounds. The stallion's eyes had been shot out. She asked the driver why these animals were in such terrible condition and was told that they had been chased by planes.

Johnston could not get the horrifying images out of her mind. When she got home, she vowed that she would do everything in her power to protect other mustangs from these inhumane acts. She complained to the U.S. Department of the Interior's Bureau of Land Management (BLM) about what she had seen. The BLM was indifferent to what Johnston had told them. She suspected that they were actually helping the ranchers and mustangers who viewed the wild horses as useless pests. Johnston became more determined than ever. She started a crusade to protect the wild horses from the poor treatment they received during aerial roundups.

Velma Johnston's efforts did not go unnoticed. Soon her opposition mockingly nicknamed her "Wild Horse Annie." Johnston liked the new name so much that she had everyone call her Annie. In 1952, Annie's efforts started to pay off. Storey County, Nevada, became the first county in the nation to make it illegal to chase wild horses by airplane.

Annie then tried to bring the plight of the wild horses to the public eye by writing magazine articles, getting signatures for petitions, and sending letters to newspapers, humane organizations, and prominent citizens. In 1955, a bill similar to the one in Storey County was passed for the state of Nevada.

Annie realized that there were wild horses in several other states, and she began to seek federal legislation. For the next several years, Annie worked closely with Walter Baring, a U.S. congressman from Nevada. In 1959, when it was time for Annie to give testimony before members of the House and Senate, her years of research paid off. Annie provided them with horrifying photographs of what happens during an aerial roundup and gave a detailed description of horse hunting. Annie explained that she and others believed that wild horses were in serious danger of becoming extinct. Annie asked Congress to protect the wild horse. She also suggested a plan of management and control of the wild-horse population so that there would be no more mass extermination programs.

Annie's testimony was so compelling that the U.S. Congress in 1959 passed a law that made it "a felony to use airplanes and motorized vehicles for rounding up unbranded wild horses on public lands." This law—the Wild Horse Annie Law—was the first federal law in America that protected wild horses.

The horses were not entirely out of danger, however. It was still legal to capture horses by horseback or trap them at water corrals and send them to slaughterhouses. As Annie had pointed out, a policy was needed to manage and control the wild-horse population. But the congressmen felt that they had done enough.

ILLEGAL ROUNDUPS

The Wild Horse Annie Law protecting wild horses from aerial round-ups was an encouraging start. Unfortunately, many mustangers defied the new law and continued to chase mustangs by air. But Annie didn't give up. In 1965, she and another Reno resident, Helen Reilly, formed an organization called The International Society for the Protection of Mustangs and Burros. They watched the BLM's activities and made the public aware of the important issues.

In 1967, Stan Routson, the supervisor of Livestock Identification for the Nevada Department of Agriculture, called Wild Horse Annie. He had been asked to act as a brand inspector for horses that had been taken on an aerial roundup. The horses were unbranded, which was a violation of federal law. They were also badly hurt, and Routson ordered them to be put out of their misery. Unfortunately, there was nothing Routson or Annie could do, because they did not actually witness the aerial roundup. But this experience convinced Routson to become a strong defender of wild horses, and he decided to help Annie in her fight.

Annie had received many anonymous calls about air hunts for wild horses. However, it was hard to prove that these aerial round-ups had taken place. According to the Bureau of Land Management, ranchers could capture branded horses, privately owned stock, with any method they wished to use—including trucks or airplanes—as long as the horses belonged to them. When ranchers were caught rounding up unbranded horses by air, they simply claimed that they were trying to round up their own horses, and the wild ones were accidentally gathered along with the domestic stock.

SPREADING THE WORD

By 1970, the mustang population was decreasing so quickly that experts predicted the horses would be extinct within ten years. Hope Ryden's book *America's Last Wild Horses*, originally published in 1972, focused public attention on the plight of the mustang. Soon details of the situation were on the front page of *The New York Times*, and the mustangs were discussed in major newspapers and on radio and TV programs. *National Geographic* magazine included a section called "On the Track of the West's Wild Horses"; *Reader's Digest* published a condensed version of Ryden's book and added a note suggesting that concerned readers write to their congressmen. *Time* magazine devoted its environment section to the wild horse.

The stories of the mustangs were so compelling that they touched the emotions of Americans all over the country. In December 1970, a fourth-grade class in Roseburg, Oregon, listened in horror as their teacher, Joan Bolsinger, described what happens to wild horses when they are corralled by airplane. The children wanted to learn more about mustangs. Miss Bolsinger told them all about the mustang: where it came from; the role it played in history; the difference in appearance between wild horses and domestic ones; and

Lynn Williams, age 10, speaks to a Senate subcommittee in 1971 about the need to protect wild horses. Fourth-grade teacher Joan Bolsinger looks on.

that so many wild horses were being killed that they might soon be extinct. The students became upset and angry. Several students called out, "There ought to be a law!" This was the beginning of a year of hard work for the Roseburg fourth graders.

The class decided to educate themselves and read all they could find about the mustang. They also wanted to learn all about Congress and how laws are passed so they could be well informed. They intended to fight for a wild-horse protection law. The students conducted a "pencil war"—they sent letters to congressmen asking them to support a law that would protect wild horses. They also wrote to schools throughout the country to gain more support for their cause. Soon children began writing to congressmen to ask them to support a wild-horse protection law.

THE SAVE-THE-HORSES BILLS

In January 1971, Gregory Gude, an eleven-year-old boy from Bethesda, Maryland, was determined to get Congress to pass a save-the-horses bill. His father was Maryland Representative Gilbert Gude. Gregory told his father all about the mustangs and asked for his help. Congressman Gude asked his son why Congress should get involved when the mustangs are found in only a few states. Greg explained that the remaining horses were a part of our history. Therefore, they were important to all Americans. Congressman Gude decided to look into the situation. He still had important questions that needed answers: Would the mustangs really die out without a law to protect them? Why weren't they already protected, like other endangered wildlife?

After a few days, Congressman Gude received a report on the mustangs from his staff. Gregory was right. The mustangs were in danger of becoming extinct if they did not receive protection soon. He found out that wild burros were also in danger of becoming extinct. The report stated that wild horses and burros were not protected because they were both classified as feral animals, not true wild animals. The report also explained that wild horses and burros live on public lands, which belong to the government of the

United States and, therefore, belong to all Americans. This information was enough to convince Congressman Gude to support a save-the-horses bill.

Congressman Gude went to see a lawyer. They drafted a bill that would give the mustang complete protection. The problem with the Wild Horse Annie Law was that it had a loophole that allowed mustangers to mix their own horses with the wild ones. Congressman Gude was going to make sure that this would not happen again. This new bill would make it illegal to mix domestic horses with wild bands. In addition, the bill stated that "all unbranded horses and burros on public lands" were to be protected, even though they were feral animals.

Gregory Gude and his father, Representative Gilbert Gude of Maryland, worked together to get many new save-the-horses bills passed by Congress.

After the save-the-horses bill was introduced in the House of Representatives, Gude had copies of the bill distributed to every senator and representative. The bill gained the support of several senators. Two of them, Republican Mark Hatfield of Oregon and Democrat Henry Jackson of Washington, decided to sponsor the bill. They introduced it in the Senate and worked hard to get the support of the people. The response was overwhelming. In fact, Senator Hatfield reported receiving as many as 25,000 letters about the mustangs in a single day.

The efforts of the media, along with those of the children across the country, were enough to get the attention of Congress. Four save-the-horses bills were introduced in the Senate, and sixteen were introduced in the House.

In April 1971, Joan Bolsinger, the Roseburg fourth-grade teacher, and Lynn Williams, one of her students, flew to Washington, D.C. They testified before committees of the House and Senate in support of the save-the-horses bills. Congressman Gude and his son Greg also testified in support of the bills, as did Wild Horse Annie.

The save-the-horses bills also had strong opponents, however. Congressman Wayne Aspinall of Colorado, who represented the ranchers, spoke out against the bills, claiming that the horses ate all the food that was meant for the sheep and cattle. Representatives of various conservation groups testified that mustangs were actually not a threat to ranchers' livestock.

There were some obstacles to the passing of the bills, which delayed the legal protection of mustangs for several more months. Congressman Aspinall and a few others who opposed the bills requested changes before the bills could be made into law. They insisted on adding amendments that would weaken the bills. Several changes were made, but the final version was still strong. The section prohibiting the mixing of domestic horses with wild ones was eliminated, but Congressman Gude still felt that the final bill was strong enough to protect the mustangs.

Finally, in December 1971, President Richard Nixon signed Public Law 92-195, the Wild Free-Roaming Horse and Burro Act. This act makes it a federal offense to harass, capture, or kill unbranded and unclaimed horses and burros. The law describes mustangs and burros as "living symbols of the historic and pioneer spirit of the West" and states that "they contribute to the diversity of life forms within the Nation and enrich the lives of the American people."

By law, the wild-horse herds would now be protected and maintained on the lands where they existed in 1971—about 300 herd areas in ten western states. Most of these lands are under the administration of the secretary of the interior, through the Bureau of Land Management; some are under the jurisdiction of the secretary of agriculture, through the Forest Service.

During the hearing, some interesting facts about the Bureau of Land Management were revealed. For years, the cattlemen and ranchers had been paying a small fee for the right to let their animals graze on public lands. When they complained that mustangs were competing with livestock for food, the BLM by law allowed the mustangers to hunt and kill the wild horses. Despite this past history, the new law placed the BLM in charge of protecting, managing, and controlling the wild, free-roaming horses and burros on public lands.

FUTURE OF THE MUSTANG

According to ranchers, the Wild Free-Roaming Horse and Burro Act has done its job too well. Since the law was enacted in 1971, the wild horses have prospered. Without their most effective predator—man—herds increased by 10 to 20 percent each year. Soon there were too many horses and too little open space. Angry ranchers blamed the horses for overgrazing and ruining the lands. Many ranchers put pressure on the Bureau of Land Management to solve the problem by reducing the number of horses.

The 1971 law, with amendments passed in 1976 and 1978, made the BLM responsible for studying the habits of wild horses and burros and the lands where they lived. One important goal of these studies was to determine an ideal size for wild-horse herds, to preserve each area's ecology and keep the multiple uses of the land—for native wildlife, the wild horses, livestock grazing, and other uses—in balance. The laws also gave the BLM the power to "manage" the herds—to humanely destroy old, sick, or lame animals when necessary, and to remove "excess" animals whose presence threatened the survival of the herd or the ecology of the area.

Protectionist groups often stood in the way of the BLM, however, and prevented them from removing any wild horses from the land. So the herds continued to grow. What the horse lovers did not realize was that in many cases they were not helping the horses. Instead, many mustangs died because of lack of food and water.

OVERPOPULATION

During the 1970s and 1980s, on the public lands on the Nevada wild-horse range at the Nellis Air Force Base north of Las Vegas, the wild-horse population was increasing rapidly. According to BLM managers, by early 1991 about 6,000 wild horses were living in an area that had enough food for only 2,000 animals. The land was in terrible condition from overgrazing. In addition, there had been a five-year drought and only enough water to support 600 animals. Many horses were dying. The BLM captured some of the horses, but were sued by the Animal Protection Institute, and the animals were not removed. To prevent further suffering, the BLM declared an emergency and removed some of the animals.

During the winters of 1990 and 1991, Spring Creek, Colorado, also experienced a similar problem. The wild-horse populations became so large that they were in danger of suffering severe food shortages. Again, although the Animal Protection Institute temporarily stopped the capture of any horses, the BLM removed some of the starving horses from the range by the spring of 1991.

Not all wild-horse groups felt the same way as the Animal Protection Institute. Judy Cady, a member of a group called Friends of the Mustangs, had a few words to say to the national preservation groups about the suffering of horses: "Get out and look. You can tell when horses are starving to death!"

ADOPT-A-HORSE PROGRAM

The Wild Free-Roaming Horse and Burro Act did not authorize the BLM to relocate wild horses to public lands if the herds did not exist there in 1971. Although the act permitted private landowners to maintain wild horses on their lands, the landowners could not take horses from public lands. So the BLM was faced with a dilemma: What to do with the excess horses?

In 1973 an Adopt-A-Horse program was tested in Montana. People could adopt a wild horse if they had an acre or two, a corral, and paid a fee. It was so successful that in 1976 the BLM began a nationwide Adopt-A-Horse program.

The Adopt-A-Horse program was a good idea, but the program was poorly managed at first, and the BLM faced much criticism. As the wild-horse populations continued to grow, the BLM captured the animals and brought them to feedlots where they were kept in corrals and holding pens. Humane groups and horse-lovers were unhappy with the BLM's method of capturing and corralling. They were rounding up the horses with helicopters, resulting in injuries.

Some of the horses that the Bureau of Land Management captured were difficult to put up for adoption. They were too old, too ugly, and bad-tempered. The BLM had to keep these horses in cattle pens, which was expensive. The penned horses lived in poor conditions, and the contractors hired by the BLM mistreated them. This situation angered animal-rights groups, and the program became highly controversial.

Adopting a Mustang

BETWEEN 6,000 and 8,000 mustangs are offered for adoption each year. Most of them are five years old or younger. The mustangs are of all colors, but sorrels, bays, and browns are the most common.

The mustangs are usually still wild, but with kindness and patience they can be trained. Some have become champions in equestrian events and racing. Each wild horse offered for adoption is examined by a veterinarian, treated for diseases, immunized, and wormed.

To adopt a wild horse, a person must be at least eighteen years old, and have no convictions for inhumane treatment of animals. He or she must also have an adequate place to keep the horse and the financial means to care for it. In some cases parents adopt the horses, and their children care for them. Young people have cared for and trained wild horses and burros as projects for 4-H, Future Farmers of America, and Scouts of America. After one year, the adopter becomes the legal owner of the mustang.

For more information about the Adopt-A-Horse program, contact the Bureau of Land Management.

A young boy test-drives an adopted wild horse belonging to a U.S. Marine Corps Mounted Color Guard at the Reno Rodeo Parade.

AN EYEWITNESS ACCOUNT

In 1977, Hope Ryden, author of *America's Last Wild Horses,* visited a Nevada site managed by the BLM to get a look at the BLM management practices. She was upset by what she saw. The horses that BLM had captured were standing in crowded corrals. Many horses had bruises and serious wounds all over their bodies from fighting. The sick and injured horses were not separated from the group. During feeding time, the strong horses quickly got to the food and ate well, and the weaker horses had to eat what was left—often little more than dirt. In addition, horses that required medical attention did not receive any help.

Some of the horses became so sick and weak that they had to be destroyed. Hope Ryden discovered that the BLM had a large gravel pit that was filled with dead mustangs of all ages. She also found eight dead horses under the age of four, and was sickened by the fact that the Adopt-A-Horse program was turning into a mass extermination program.

In 1978, the American Horse Protection Association sued the BLM, arguing that the large numbers of horse removals were not necessary. Hope Ryden was asked to testify on her experiences at the BLM site. The outcome of the trial was that the BLM improved their management practices and eliminated many previous abuses.

Between the 1970s and 1990s, the Adopt-A-Horse program arranged for the adoption of more than 130,000 horses. During the 1980s, however, it was discovered that some people who hauled away large numbers of horses ("lot adopters") were actually ranchers who were sending the horses to be slaughtered. The law required that a person could adopt only four horses in a single year.

Wild horses corralled at the Bureau of Land Management, awaiting adoption.

The ranchers gave the names of family members, each of whom was listed as adopting four horses. After a one-year holding period, the ranchers had legal ownership of the horses and were free to do whatever they wanted with them.

The BLM was taken to court by the animal-rights groups Fund for Animals and Animal Protection Institute of America. The threat of a lawsuit put a stop to "lot adoptions" by ranchers. The BLM was held responsible for violating the Wild Free-Roaming Horse and Burro Act by giving the horses to people whose intentions were to "exploit and destroy them."

The BLM began efforts to improve the adoption program. New adoption centers were opened, which made horses available to people in other parts of the country. One was set up at a Colorado prison so that prisoners could halter the wild horses (train the horses to wear a halter). Many buyers had refused to adopt the mustangs because they were so unmanageable, so this program helped to make the horses more appealing. Prisoners who were close to release or posed no security risk were selected for the program. The program was like a form of rehabilitation for the prisoners, teaching them patience and responsibility. Between 1985 and 1988, about 1,100 horses were tamed and put up for adoption. The prisoner program was expanded to include saddle training and now exists in California, New Mexico, and Wyoming.

HYDE TO THE RESCUE

Dayton Hyde has dedicated his life to helping animals and preserving wildlife. In 1958, Hyde bought his uncle's 5,000-acre (2,000-hectare) cattle ranch in Oregon and leased another 85,000 acres (35,000 hectares), which he also managed. Like generations of cowboys, Hyde caught and broke (tamed) mustangs and rode them to herd his cattle. Sometimes when he found starving horses roaming on public lands, he drove them to better pastures on his ranch.

By the mid-1980s, Hyde had spoken to various organizations to encourage support for the wild-horse protection effort. In 1988, Hyde was saddened and concerned when he heard that the BLM was keeping wild horses in feedlots. To reduce the growing number of

Dayton Hyde
with wild horses
living in the
sanctuary.

wild horses waiting in BLM holding facilities, Hyde suggested that the excess horses be placed in privately owned sanctuaries. He felt that private landowners would be able to manage wild horses better than government agencies.

Hyde formed an organization called the Institute of Range and the American Mustang (IRAM). He and his organization set up two mustang refuges in South Dakota. He raised the money for a 11,000-acre (4,453-hectare) site located in the Black Hills (west of Hot Springs). A group of private investors bought a 35,000-acre (14,165-hectare) site for almost two million dollars and allowed IRAM to use it. The BLM made an agreement with Hyde to place 2,000 wild horses on the two sanctuaries. Hyde would manage the horses and provide extra feed and medical care when necessary. The BLM paid IRAM about a dollar per day for each of the horses. To keep each horse on the feedlots would cost more than two dollars per day. In order to pay for the increasing expenses and mortgage payments, Hyde opened the 11,000-acre site to tourists in 1990, charging a fee for guided tours.

The refuges seemed so successful that the BLM decided to support another wild-horse sanctuary in Bartlesville, Oklahoma, which opened in 1989. Hyde's larger refuge eventually closed, but the Hot Springs sanctuary is now financially self-sufficient, operating with volunteer help and without federal funds. The mustangs roam freely on the sanctuaries and form bands just as they do in the wild. Hyde says that they are "fat and sassy," but they still panic when a helicopter flies by.

BIRTH CONTROL FOR HORSES

Removing adult horses from the wild herds has not been an effective means of reducing the mustang populations. BLM biologists have discovered that in the years after each roundup of horses for adoption, the birthrate in the remaining herd increases up to 100 percent. Soon the herd is back up to its previous size and continues to grow at the rate of about 15 to 20 percent a year. The herd can double in size in just four years!

The horses taken for the adoption program are often the youngest, healthiest, most attractive members of the herd, because they are the ones most likely to be adopted. But as the best horses are continually removed, offspring of the wild herds tend to have unattractive characteristics and unhealthy genetic makeup. Biologically, this is a poor way to "manage" an animal population.

The latest effort to reduce wild-horse populations has been fertility control (prevention of reproduction), which is intended to decrease the number of excess births. Between 1992 and 1994, a contraceptive vaccine, called Porcine Zonae Pellucida (PZP) was tested on herds in Nevada. The objective of the project was to make mares temporarily unable to conceive. The drug works by causing the female's body to reject its own eggs. The study involved giving the mares two injections within four weeks. However, the horses had to be corralled for as long as a month, which made them susceptible to disease and decreased their wildness. Therefore, the plan did not work.

In 1996, field testing of an improved contraceptive vaccine began on about 400 mares at the Nevada Wild Horse Range. The new vaccine is said to require a single shot, and the effects last for a year. The question was: Is it worth the effort for just one year's protection? According to BLM biologist Kris Eshelman, each horse born on the range, captured, and adopted, costs the taxpaying public about $1,000. The cost of gathering the horses and injecting the vaccine is estimated at less than $300. So each prevention of a birth saves the public $700.

ARE HORSE REMOVALS NECESSARY?

At the end of 1995, the wild-horse population was a little more than 35,500. More than 130,000 mustangs had been placed with private owners in the Adopt-A-Horse program. But BLM biologists say that there are still too many horses in many areas; the "appropriate management level" for the mustang population on the 41.5 million acres (16.8 million hectares) of public lands where they are found is estimated at 23,500.

Compare the BLM target population for the mustangs to the current numbers for the desert bighorn sheep. The sheep, with a population of about 50,000, was declared an endangered species, and extensive efforts were made to increase its numbers. Kris Eshelman of the BLM comments that endangered species populations such as the bighorn are decreasing or barely holding their own, and that mustangs, if left alone, have the potential to increase their numbers by 20 percent a year.

For years, the wild-horse populations have been held partially responsible for overgrazing the western lands. Ranchers have accused horses of destroying vegetation, causing erosion, and polluting waters. As Hope Ryden has pointed out, however, about 4,350,000 domestic livestock graze on these public lands. In addition, about 2,000,000 antelope, deer, elk, and other large wild animals share these lands. The 35,500 or so wild horses represent less than 1 percent of the large grazing animals on the western lands. Could they really be responsible for all the damage to the habitat? she asks.

Why do mustangs continue to be considered a nuisance? Is it really necessary to reduce wild populations that are already at low numbers? Mustangs are a symbol of freedom to the American people. For that reason alone, aren't they worth preserving?

Wild horse, running free in Montana.

FINGERTIP FACTS

Height	Adult mustangs generally grow to about 58 inches (147 centimeters) at the withers (between the shoulders), although height can vary from 3 to 5 feet (0.9 to 1.5 meters).
Weight	Adult mustangs weigh an average of about 1,000 pounds (450 kilograms).
Color	Mustangs have a variety of colors and patterns of colors: bay (reddish brown coat), sorrel (yellowish brown coat), chestnut, black, gray, roan (solid-colored coat with white hair scattered throughout), palomino (golden body with white mane and tail), buckskin (yellowish gray coat), paint (two-colored coat with white and black or brown), and Appaloosa (white patch on rump with small dark spots).
Food	Mustangs feed primarily on grass and shrubs.
Reproduction	Females are ready to breed when they are a year old; most males are not ready to breed until they are two to three years old, and sometimes even older. Females typically give birth to one foal in the spring after a gestation period of 11 months.

Care for young	Foals depend on the mother's milk for the first three to four weeks of life. They then feed on grass and nurse less often. At four to five months they no longer need their mother's milk. Both parents protect the young, and the stallion acts as a disciplinarian. However, the male will sacrifice the young if they are hampering a quick getaway.
Range	Mustangs live in ten western states. The largest numbers are in Nevada (about 26,000). Other states, such as Idaho, Oregon, Wyoming, Colorado, New Mexico, and California have herds numbering from 1,500 to 4,000. Mustangs are also found in Montana, Utah, and Arizona.
Population size	In 1996 about 30,500 mustangs were living in the wild.
Social behavior	Mustangs are sociable animals that live in bands all year.
Life span	Mustangs can live up to 20 years or more in the wild.

FURTHER READING

Books

Berger, Joel. *Wild Horses of the Great Basin: Social Competition and Population Size.* Chicago: The University of Chicago Press, 1986.

Eustin-Cross, Barbara, and Bowker, Nancy. *The Wild Horse: An Adopter's Manual.* New York: Macmillan, 1992.

Roever, J. M. and Wilfred. *The Mustangs.* Austin, TX: Steck-Vaughn, 1971.

Ryden, Hope. *America's Last Wild Horses,* rev. ed. New York: Lyons & Burford, 1990.

Ryden, Hope. *A Return to the Wild.* New York: The Viking Press, 1972.

Weiss, Ann. *Save the Mustangs! How a Federal Law Is Passed.* New York: Simon and Schuster, 1974.

Pamphlet

"America's Wild Horses & Burros: Managing a Living Legend," Reno, NV: Bureau of Land Management, 1987.

Articles

Berger, Joel, "Funding Asymmetries for Endangered Species, Feral Animals, and Livestock," *BioScience,* February 1991, pp. 105-106.

Foote, Donna, "Death on the Range," *Newsweek,* July 22, 1991, p. 25.

"No Longer Home on the Open Range," *U.S. News and World Report,* June 13, 1988, pp. 57-58.

Symanski, Richard, "America's Wild Horses," *Focus,* Fall 1986, pp. 20-28.

Tennesen, Michael, "Reining in a Runaway Herd," *National Wildlife,* October/November 1992, pp. 22-25.

"Wild Horse Refuge," *Encyclopedia Science Supplement 1993.* New York: Franklin Watts, 1992, pp. 291-296.

Williamson, Lonnie, "Out of Range," *Outdoor Life,* April 1992, pp. 96-98.

Internet Resources

http://iquest.com/~jhines/mustang/general.html (The Wild Horse, Mustang & Burro Page)

http://www.webcom.com/~ladyhawk/Colors1.html (Pryor Mountain Wild Horse Refuge)

http://www.horseworld.com/imh/ (International Museum of the Horse; an extensive on-line history of the horse)

http://www.aesir.com/CWHF/Welcome.html (Corolla Wild Horse Fund)

http://www.nando.net/ncd/week15/carova2.html (Northern Outer Banks Wild Horse Sanctuary)

http://www.freerein.com/breeds.html/haynet (The Hay.net; an exhaustive list of horse sites on the Internet)

http://www.blm.gov/whb/ (Official National Wild Horse and Burro site)

ORGANIZATIONS

American Feral Horse Association
4820 Allamar
Boise, ID 83704
(208) 375-1384

American Mustang Association
P.O. Box 338
Yucaipa, CA 92399

American Mustang & Burro Association, Inc.
P.O. Box 788
Lincoln, CA 95648
(916) 633-9271

American Mustang & Burro Association, Inc.
P.O. Box 216
Liberty Hill, TX 78642
(800) US-4-WILD

Bureau of Land Management
National Wild Horse and Burro Program Office
850 Harvard Way
P.O. Box 12000
Reno, NV 89520-0006
(702) 785-6583

Corolla Wild Horse Fund of
Outer Banks Conservationists
P.O. Box 361
Corolla, NC 27927

Friends of the Mustangs
c/o Judy Cady
2131 L-½ Road
Grand Junction, CO 81505

H.L. Hollingsworth
R.R. 4, Box 95
Marshall, IL 62441
(217) 826-2405

International Society for the Protection
of Mustangs & Burros (ISPMB)
6212 East Sweetwater Avenue
Scottsdale, AZ 85254
(602) 991-0273

Middle Tennessee Mustang Association
P.O. Box 1671
Lavergne, TN 37086
(615) 793-3776

National Mustang Association, Inc.
1st and Main Streets
Newcastle, UT 84756
(801) 439-5440

National Organization for Wild Horses, Inc.
1330 South 9th Street
Canon City, CO 81212
(719) 275-1142

North American Mustang Association & Registry
P.O. Box 850906
Mesquite, TX 75185-0906
(214) 289-9344

Steens Mountain Kiger Registry
26450 Horsell
Bend, OR 97701
(541) 389-3895

Tri-State Mustang Club
RR1, Box 180
Hayfield, MN 55940
(507) 477-2676

INDEX